The Complete Guide to
RESEARCHING and WRITING the
English Term Paper

The Complete Guide to RESEARCHING and WRITING the English Term Paper

by Allan Blondé

Chairman, English Department
Holy Cross High School
Flushing, New York 11358

Published by Scholium International Inc.
130-30 31st Avenue
Flushing, New York 11354

Library of Congress Catalogue Card Number 78-63036
ISBN 0-87936-013-5

Contents

1 PRIMARY SOURCE SELECTION 1
2 CRITICAL APPROACHES TO LITERATURE. 3
3 TYPES OF CRITICAL BOOKS. 15
4 BIBLIOGRAPHY WORK 23
5 HOW TO TAKE NOTES 33
6 HOW TO ORGANIZE NOTE CARDS. 37
7 WRITING THE PAPER: COMPOSITION 43
8 WRITING THE PAPER: MECHANICS. 50
9 AFTER WRITING THE PAPER 56

APPENDIX A: PRIMARY SOURCE LIST. 59
APPENDIX B: SAMPLE NOTES PAGE. 67

Preface to the Teacher

There are many guides to the writing of the research paper currently available. However, the present guide has a number of distinct features which distinguishes it from all others.

First, because the guide specifically aims at teaching the English research paper, it is able to concern itself with the entire process of researching and writing the paper. Even before bibliography work is discussed considerable time is spent on types of literary criticism and the kinds of critical books available. This information is included with the hope that the student will be able to intelligently understand the criticism he is reading, as well as to be able to enact the more mechanical procedures for the writing of a term paper.

Secondly, the chapter on the critical approaches to literature may be used by the teacher who wishes to include the various modes of literary criticism as kerygma for the interpretation of any literature to be covered by the course he is teaching.

A third distinguishing characteristic of this manual is its insistence on the objective nature of literary criticism. Hopefully, the use of the manual will act as a corrective against the fact that the necessity for logic, exactness, and supporting data, which is so much a part of scientific inquiry, is often lost sight of by those approaching the more personal meaning of literature.

Lastly, this guide moves beyond delineating only the major mechanics of the term paper, such as how to write an introduction and conclusion, or how to organize the notes page, by including recommendations for the complete format of the paper down to the smallest details of its binding and pagination, and, by including in each case, the reason for employment of each technique, so that the student understands why it is better to use the outlined procedure.

The cordial reception given during the last few years to the ideas and methods outlined in this manual by my own students, if given only after they have "run the gauntlet," leads me to believe that its contents can be of some use to others who have the task of introducing the student to the techniques of research writing about literature.

Preface to the Student

This guide is designed to assist you in a step by step production of the term paper. You will first learn some general rules for selecting a research paper topic and obtain the necessary background in the science of literary criticism. After that you will be ready to study the process of constructing a critical bibliography and of notetaking. Finally, both the composition and the more mechanical aspects of the actual writing of the paper will be discussed. The procedures used in these notes have been tested over a period of many years and many of them are the most standard ways of researching and writing the paper. There are other ways of writing the research paper, but if you learn this method it should serve you well throughout your college career, as well as have the more immediate effect of making you more critical in your thinking about literature.

1
Primary Source Selection

SELECTING A TOPIC

The literary work or works that a research paper is about is called the *primary source*, since it is the first thing you must look at when undertaking the writing of a paper. Because the paper will be basically a researching of what the critics have said about the literary work you have chosen for your topic, it is essential to keep in mind a few general rules about the selection of the topic. First, don't select any work that is too recent. If the work has been written in the last twenty years or so it is quite likely that literary critics have not yet written much about it. Certainly it will not have had a chance for making the various kinds of standard critical books which will be discussed later. This will make your research of criticism of the work difficult if not impossible. Secondly, don't select a work whose meaning is so obvious that it has never required any response from the critics. Works such as *War of the Worlds* by H. G. Wells, or *Treasure Island* by Robert Louis Stevenson may be interesting to read, but they are not complex or puzzling enough to have required anybody's critical response and, therefore, would be difficult to do research on. Thirdly, avoid selecting a topic that you are totally unfamiliar with. Some students waste time finding out they really are not sufficiently interested in their chosen topic to motivate them to spend the necessary time and energy researching it. A generally good procedure is to check out the work you have selected by going to one of the standard reference plot summary books such as *Masterplots,* which can be found in almost any library. Fourthly, be sure to select something that you are actually going to read. In addition to being tested in the work once you have read it, a thorough familiarity of the work will be essential if you are to read the critics intelligently. A vague recollection of the work will make it impossible to completely understand or agree or disagree with the criticism you will be reading about the work.

For your convenience an appendix has been attached to these notes which consists of a list of possible research paper choices. This list is not only a compilation of very popular books, but is the result of a survey taken among college instructors throughout the country. They were asked to list books they considered important enough for the student to have read before coming to college. The list is a compilation of their responses.

Finally, feel free to consult with your instructor about a choice of topic. He will most likely be familiar with the criticism available and be able to assist you in your selection.

Assignment: Make a list of five possible *primary source* choices.
#1   List them in the order of your preference.

The instructor will then approve of one of the topics on the basis of what everybody has requested. It will be impossible to approve too many students for the same topic because the same critical materials will later be needed by all those with that topic.

Review Question: Can you now recall what four ideas you must remember to make an intelligent primary source choice?

2

Critical Approaches to Literature

INTRODUCTION TO LITERARY CRITICISM

The Five Critical Approaches

If one surveys the field of *literary criticism*, i.e., the scientific analysis of literature, one finds that almost all criticism is written from one of five basic points of view. I believe it will be of some interest, as well as provide you with a greater degree of understanding, to discuss the historical origins of each of these approaches. There are three advantages to knowing something about these "approaches." First, it is impossible for you to write in your research paper all that can be said about the literary work you have selected as your primary source. Knowing about the various critical approaches and selecting one of these to work with will be one way to limit your topic to a more manageable size. Secondly, knowledge of the approaches will help you while you are doing the actual researching for the paper by permitting you to disregard some of the critics, or at least some of what they have said, from critical points of view that you are not interested in. This cuts down significantly on the amount of reading you must do and makes the task of doing a thorough research job within reach of everyone. The third advantage of knowing about the approaches is one that applies to your reading of literature outside of the research paper assignment. Frequently the student is puzzled as to the meaning of a piece of literature after he has read it. Knowledge of the various critical approaches will permit you to make an intelligent attempt at understanding the meaning and will increase your perception of the value of the literature that you read.

The First Two Approaches

An examination of the earliest attempts at literature in almost any cultural tradition indicates that early man was principally concerned with writing about two kinds of information. Early works such as the *Bible* or the Homeric poems the *Iliad* and the *Odyssey* were composed in large part even before the invention of writing and were laboriously memorized by each generation so that they could be transmitted to their children and their children's children. Even after writing was invented reading these books became the basic method for each respective civilization to educate its young. It is, therefore, natural to ask what these works contained that was so important for the people to place so much emphasis on them. This investigative curiosity is the beginning of literary criticism. The desire to analyze and dissect a work of literature in order to obtain a more precisely defined idea or set of ideas about it is *the basic attitude of the critic* or, indeed, of anyone who wishes to advance beyond the stage of just having a vague, incommunicable, and consequently untrustworthy "idea" about a piece of literature he has read.

To return to the more specific purpose at hand, if one analyzes these early literary works one finds that they are basically about two things. First, they attempt to explain why things happen the way they do; that is, they probe toward a naming and understanding of the ultimate nature of reality. This attitude or study of "the ultimate being," to use a philosophical phrase, is what is called theology. Once one has obtained some idea of the nature of reality at large it is far easier to determine the purpose of human existence; and once this has been decided it is only a short step to constructing a set of rules or ideals about how man should act in order to reach his goal or fulfill his purpose according to the general and ultimate nature of things. The study of man's ideals is what is meant by the term "ethics" or "morality." Therefore, it is not surprising to find that in the same works of literature that discuss the theological nature of things there is a great deal of ethical information about how man should act. The key word in this point of view is the word "should," because, first, it implies that we are talking about an ideal situation in contrast to the way things now are, and, secondly, it implies that man has the obligation to shoot for that level of activity. In turn, the obligation suggests that man is able to make this ideal attempt, or that he is "free" to put his ideals into practice.

Consequently, two critical approaches to literature quickly became the standard ways of commenting on and understanding what the literature of the time was about. The first of these was the *Theological Approach* which can be defined as "an investigation of literature that analyzes what the work has to say about the ultimate nature of things or why things are the way they are." Closely related to this approach and often used by the critic in the same book in which he takes a theological approach is the *Ethical or Moral Approach*. This approach may be defined as "an investigation of literature which analyzes what the work has to say about how man should act or which analyzes the nature of human ideals or of human freedom."

A quick survey of literature from the earliest literary works written, such as those already mentioned, to those written as late as the fourteenth century A.D. indicates that almost all of them can be approached either theologically and/or ethically. One or two examples will make this clear. Dante's famous medieval work *The Divine Comedy,* which tells the story of the poet being guided through the regions of hell, purgatory, and heaven, clearly indicates that the ultimate nature of things includes a divine being who metes out absolute justice. Just as clearly the book is about ethical matters because it clearly illustrates the punishments or rewards associated with various forms of human behavior. Similarly, Chaucer's *Canterbury Tales,* a description of a group of pilgrims on their way to Canterbury Cathedral, can be investigated for its comment on the ethics of each of the pilgrims, or, on a more subtle level, the implication about the theological matter of salvation and divine mercy.

Two Nineteenth Century Approaches

The coming of modern science during the Renaissance (14th-16th centuries) was to have a profound effect upon the literary imagination and, consequently, upon the way in which literature would be interpreted. On a theoretical level science insisted upon explaining things in terms of cause and effect. Why do the stars move across the heavens the way they do? Why do the tides come in and go out at predictable times each day? Why are the birds able to fly? And the answer was always *"because."* The literature of the Renaissance responded to this notion of cause and effect almost immediately. This can be seen in many of the plays of Shakespeare. Why, for example, does Macbeth kill Duncan and enter upon a life of crime? *Because* he is living in an atmosphere of rebellion which establishes itself at the opening of the play. *Because* he lives in Scotland where the persistently bad weather has a negative effect upon the mind. *Because* he has the seeds of the murder planted in him by the prediction of the witches. *Because* his shrewish wife, Lady Macbeth, urges, cajoles, and pursuades him to do the crime.

What is important to notice in the above illustration is that all of the forces acting upon Macbeth have an almost absolute causal effect upon him, making him a slave to these forces rather than a free man. Thus, the notion of man as a free moral being begins to be replaced by the notion of man as a psychological being; that is, somebody whose actions can be explained in terms of causal influences. This notion was temporarily placed in the background during the 17th and 18th centuries when science and, consequently, literature became concerned principally with the external, physical world rather than man. However, when the Romantic revolution against this external disposition came at the end of the 18th century, literature and science once again addressed themselves to the question of how man's mind operates; that is, what kinds of causes influence behavior. By the middle of the nineteenth century a new science, modern psychology, had arrived on the scene and with it came an avalanche of literature concerned with the portrayal of psychological rather than moral man. The science of psychology was reinforced by modern biology, which was also making its debut at about the same time and which attempted to explain man in terms of internal, or genetic, and external, or environmental, forces or causes.

A book such as Crane's *The Red Badge of Courage* shows clearly the effect of this new view of man. The title of the book is ironic, of course, because the Youth who is the protagonist is not a morally courageous person. Rather his actions are dictated by a response to internal fears caused by external conditions. Thus, Crane's book becomes part of a new literary genre the "psychological novel." At about the same time authors like Poe sought to give miniaturized psychological portraits of persons in his short stories.

With the advent of a body of literature concerning itself with psychological man, the psychological approach to literature came into existence. *The Psychological Approach* can be defined as "an investigation of literature that analyzes the motives of the characters in the literary work." The psychological approach requires the abandonment of the notion of freedom as an explanation of man's behavior and, thus, replaces or is antagonistic to the moral approach.

Just as science caused the replacing of a moral view of man with a psychological view it also indirectly caused the replacement of theological concerns with a concern for more mundane matters. The application of scientific theory produced new techniques, or a technology, for dealing with the material world. For the first time more than just a very small segment of the population was able to attain an economically good status. The 17th and 18th centuries saw the rise of the middle class and, with the coming of the industrial revolution in the middle of the 18th century, the lower class began to revolute into economic prominence. The new economic status conferred upon the average man gave him a new social importance and this, in turn, stimulated the coming of new or revived social sciences in the nineteenth century. History, the story of collective rather than individual man, came into bold relief in the nineteenth century. Similarly, the new social science of sociology came into being to consider the socio-economic problems of collective man.

Literature, too, responded to these new interests. The nineteenth century realized an unbelievably large number of novels and plays that addressed themselves to economic and social problems of the time. From about 1830 to 1880 Charles Dickens' novels and short stories explored the problems of poverty and family life in England. Here in the United States Mark Twain considered the problems of the poor in his novel *The Prince and The Pauper* and later, in *Huckleberry Finn* he addressed himself to the problem of social integration between the races. In 1850 Henryk Ibsen, who was to become named "The Father of Modern Drama" because of his new interests in social problems, began a series of plays that were later termed "social problem plays."

Criticism, too, responded to the situation. A new critical approach came into existence. Not surprisingly, it was named *The Historical or Sociological Approach* to literature. It can be defined as "an investigation of literature that analyzes one of two relationships existing between the literary work and history or society." First, the approach may analyze how the historical or social conditions of the time in which the author lived influenced the writing of the work; and, secondly, it may analyze how the work influenced history or society. Referring once again to the novels of Dickens we can see how this works. The critic might approach any of his novels by analyzing how the work reflects the social concerns of middle nineteenth century England. Essentially what the critic is doing here is showing how the literary work is a product of its time; in the case of Dickens how his novels are "Victorian" in nature. This is perhaps the easiest approach to take with any literary work and, although it came into prominence as a result of nineteenth century literature, it can easily be applied to almost any literary work from any historical time period. Thus, *Canterbury Tales* can be approached as a description of medieval society; or *Macbeth* can be analyzed in terms of the Renaissance concern about what constitutes a good king. Because every literary work is the product of an author who is, at least to some degree, influenced by the time in which he lives, every literary work can be approached historically or sociologically.

Besides demonstrating how society or social conditions influenced the writing of a work, the historical approach may also examine how the work influenced society. The publication of Upton Sinclair's *The Jungle,* for example, was so scathing an indictment of the unsanitary conditions in the meat packing industry that the book stimulated public opinion to such an extent that legislation was passed to improve the conditions in that industry. Often, however, the way in which a literary work affects any given social situation is very subtle, making it difficult to use this specific type of historical approach with any great degree of evidence about one's conclusions.

Two Twentieth Century Approaches

Although literature responded to the new concerns of man in the nineteenth century, namely that of psychology and the social sciences, there was an increasing belief that literature could not really compete with science for communicating the hard facts that modern man was interested in. Increasingly, literature began to be seen simply as entertainment rather than a vehicle for truth and knowledge. This was reinforced by the fact that most literature written prior to the nineteenth century was about theological or moral matters which no longer occupied man's central interests. In order to save literature from total disregard critics began a search for a new way of approaching literature. The approach would have to cite some value that belonged to literature alone and which could not be snatched away by the increasing domain of the sciences. A new formula was arrived at by Walter Pater, an art historian who also had literary interests. He claimed that literature did not have as its purpose the transmitting of any kind of information, but, instead, it was the function of literature to produce pleasure in the reader by being a thing of beauty. Thus Pater stated that literature does not exist for the sake of theology, ethics, psychology, history, or any other subject area; rather literature, indeed, all art exists only for its own sake. Thus the *Aesthetic Approach* to literature, whose central doctrine is "Art for the Sake of Art" was arrived at.

However, if the critic did not analyze the literary work to see what it had to say about a given subject, what would be the point of the critical analysis? The answer supplied by the Aesthetic critic was that the critic would analyze not what the work said, but rather how the work was constructed. It was the Aesthetic critics' belief that the structure or form of the work is the quality that makes the work entertaining and, therefore, worthwhile to the reader. Thus, the *Aesthetic or Formal Approach* can be defined as "an investigation of literature which analyzes how the work is structured." In particular, it was observed that the basic structure of all art, as well as of all natural objects, rests on the notion of repetition. Just as twentieth century physics was discovering that all material objects repeated the basic ingredients called atoms, so too, literature could be analyzed as a series of repetitions.

Perhaps an example will make this clear. The literary critic who uses an Aesthetic or Formal approach might analyze the effectiveness of the first line of Blake's famous poem "The Tyger" (Tyger, tyger, burning bright) by pointing out the repetitions of three two syllable words in sequence, or by showing the repetition of the "t," hard "g," or "b" sounds. Further, he might point out that all three of those sounds are similar because they are all the products of making an explosive noise with our articulators, which are all called "plosive sounds." The critic might conclude his brief analysis with the fact the syllabic repetition produces a very defined rhythm which is nothing more or less than a series of sounds made at repetitive intervals.

The Aesthetic approach to literature and art in general has been pervasive in the twentieth century. The point of view behind MGM's film release *That's Entertainment* was already formed when the company took as part of its trademark around the head of Leo the Lion the phrase "Ars Gratia Artis," "Art for the Sake of Art." It might be said, without exaggeration, that the great majority of the people who read literature today are reading for entertainment or pleasure alone and, as such, are assuming the effects, if not the critical awareness, of the Aesthetic or Formal critic.

One of the ways in which imaginative writers indicated that literature was not to be used for information was to write about subjects which were, at least apparently, meaningless. One such area was the fantasy world of dreams. One outstanding example of this is Lewis Carroll's *Alice in Wonderland*. Not only is the work at large apparently meaningless, but specific sections, such as the "Jabbawocky" poem seem to be pure nonsense. At about the same time, as psychology made headway in the nineteenth century, psychologists turned their attention more and more to people with emotional problems and who didn't make sense all of the time. One man in particular, Sigmund Freud, sought to find the key to interpreting the actions and psychological situations of his mentally disturbed patients. Through a combination of hard work and accident Freud hit upon the answer. If dreams were taken seriously they could be used to discover the causes of psychological illness. In a massive work published in 1900, *The Interpretation of Dreams,* Freud discussed dream symbolism and the mechanisms of the unconscious. While working on one of his most famous theories Freud noticed that literature, especially the kind thought to be meaningless, those ancient literary works that were once interpreted theologically, could now be used to illustrate how the unconscious operates and what it was like because this literature used the same symbolic code that showed up in people's dreams.

By showing the correspondence between the symbols that the unconscious produced and those used in literary works Freud unwitingly discovered a new critical approach to literature. This new approach, the ***Psychoanalytic Approach***, restored to literature its content meaning and has become, in the twentieth century, the chief opponent of Formal criticism which denies that literature means anything of value. With the psychoanalytic approach one may investigate literature as a symbolic code which attempts to inform us about the nature of the human mind, especially that part which is impossible to observe directly known as the unconscious. ***The Psychoanalytic Approach*** may, therefore, be defined as "an investigation of literature that analyzes what the work has to say about the structure of the mind and how the unconscious, in particular, operates."

Perhaps you will recall that this section of the notes was entitled the five critical approaches. Yet we have just defined the sixth. The discrepancy can be easily cleared up. It was noticed almost immediately after psychoanalytic criticism started to be written that it was very similar to theological criticism. The same symbols within a given literary work that could be understood theologically could be also understood or interpreted psychoanalytically. In addition, the purpose of a theo-

logical interpretation was to arrive at a clearer idea of the ultimate objective meaning of things. This purpose was very similar
to psychoanalytic criticism which investigated literature to arrive at a clearer idea of the ultimate subjective meaning of
things, that is, the human mind. The two approaches were,
therefore, combined and are today known as the *Mythological
or Archetypal Approach.* The approach is called "mythological"
because the literature that is investigated is always mythic in
character and it is called "archetypal" because the literature investigated always has archetypes, or universally used symbols,
by which to relate the mythic story.

When using or discussing the mythological approach it is always good, however, to specifically add (for the sake of clarity)
which sub-approach, theological or psychoanalytic, you are
using.

One last question remains. How do you, the reader, know
which approach is most suitable for any given work? First, keep
in mind that more than one approach may be used with a particular work. Literature is by nature ambiguous. It does not
mean just one thing. A great work of literature will invite criticism from many different points of view and will reveal a many
faceted wisdom. Homer's *Odyssey,* for example, can be interpreted theologically because it speaks about gods and other
fantastical beings. But because these beings may be interpreted
as symbols of the mind, the book can also be approached psychoanalytically. In addition, the book yields a considerable
amount of information about how early Greek society operated
and, therefore, a historical approach would also be a profitable
undertaking. Lastly, the presence of repetitive patterns throughout the work invites commentary from a formal point of view.
However, one easy way to determine which approach to use is
simply to ask yourself what the literary work is about. Limit
your answer to one simple sentence so that you get down to an
essential description of the work. Now analyze your answer. It
will most likely contain one or more key words that can be as-

sociated to one or more of the approaches. If your first description doesn't seem to yield any clues to the work's meaning, state another description and check it for key words.

An example will illustrate this process. If one reads *The Scarlet Letter* by Hawthorne and describes it as "a story about people who feel guilty about their sins," the words "guilty" and "sins" immediately suggest a psychological and theological or ethical interpretation. Also keep in mind that one could always take a historical approach to the work showing, for example, how it has all of the characteristics of a typical Romantic novel: that is, how the novel reflects the qualities of the Romantic era in the history of literature.

Assignment: As you read your primary source attempt to guess
#2   which approach or approaches have been used by
                  the critics by determining the approaches yourself.
                  Determine, if possible, which approach you feel
                  is best suited or most revealing of the work's
                  meaning.

Review Questions:

1.   Can you name and define the five approaches to literary criticism?
2.   Can you explain in your own words how and why each approach came into existence?
3.   Can you explain which procedure is used to determine which approach or approaches are suitable for use with a given literary work?

3

Types of Critical Books

DIFFERENT TYPES OF BOOKS
DISTINGUISHED BY THEIR SCOPE

Critical books not only differ in the point of view or critical approach that the author takes but also by the amount of territory or scope that the particular critical book covers. Some critics write a book that comments on a vast number of literary works, while others will concentrate an entire book of criticism on one literary work. It is important for the person beginning to do research to know what kind of material can be found in what kind of book and the order in which to read these various kinds of books.

The first kind of book that should be consulted when doing research is a book which covers the *General History of the Literature of a Country*. Such a book as Baugh's *A Literary History of England* surveys the entire field of English literature. The reasons for consulting this type of book first is, that it gives the most elementary information about each literary work as well as the most widely accepted critical ideas. The reason for this is that the author of this type of book knows that the book will be used by those just getting acquainted with criticism, so he has to write something that will be elementary enough for everyone to understand and he also has the obligation of communicating the most widely accepted critical ideas to the novice who as yet is unable to distinguish between good and bad critical ideas.

Other important examples of general histories are

A Literary History of the U.S. by Spiller et al. (and others),
The Cambridge History of English Literature, edited by
    Ward and Waller, a fifteen volume work,
The Oxford History of English Literature, a several volume
    work by several authors,
Spiller's *Cycles of American Literature,*
Kazin's *On Native Ground,* and
Howard's *Literature and the American Tradition.*

I have listed only books about British and American literature since that is the type of literature most students will be
working on. However, works such as these can be found about
the literature of almost every major country.

The reader will note that dictionaries and encyclopedias
have not been listed even though they are general books which
might very well discuss a great number of literary works and
authors. The reason that they are not included is because they
are designed not to critically comment on the works of literature but simply to give facts about the work and the author. As
such they are of little use to the researcher of literary criticism.
A good general policy is, therefore, never to use any general
books of this type.

Once you have consulted one or more general histories of
literature you will know enough about the work and about the
critical ideas related to it to encounter books that explore specific literary works more thoroughly. Two types of books which
are more specific than the general history book are **genre books**
and **era books**. One way that a critic limits the scope of his work
so that he can spend more time commenting on each specific
literary work is by discussing only works of a certain genre or
type of literature, such as poetry, drama, the short story, or the
novel. Frequently genre books will not discuss every single literary work of a given country even in the particular genre, but
will, instead, sample certain works from a number of countries.

Just as frequently some genre books will limit their discussion to only a certain number of literary works within the genre. The general principle that applies here, as well as to all types of critical books, is that the smaller the scope, that is, the fewer the number of literary works discussed by the critic, the more in-depth will be the critic's discussion of each work.

Here is a list of some of the more famous genre books:

Allen, *The English Novel*
Bush, *An Outline of English Poetry*
Gassner, *Masters of the Drama*
Kettle, *An Introduction to the English Novel* (2 vols.)
Drew, *The Novel: A Modern Guide to Fifteen English Masterpieces*
Fergussen, *The Idea of the Theatre*
O'Conner, *The Lonely Voice* (on the Short Story)
Muller, *The Spirit of Tragedy*
Sewall, *The Vision of Tragedy*
Bush, *Science and English Poetry*

The last three examples listed illustrate ways in which the author will make his genre book even more specific. In the Muller and Sewall books the author has limited himself to discussing a certain sub-genre of drama, namely tragedy. On the other hand, Bush's book indicates that the author is not going to discuss poetry in general, but only those poems which specifically relate to science. These are just a few examples of an almost infinite variety of ways in which to make the critical book even more specific than a simple genre book.

A type of book that is about as general as the genre book is the book which limits itself to talking about literary works only in one particular literary era. Thus the critic might discuss only Medieval literature, or only Romantic literature, or only Modern literature. You should already be familiar with the various major literary eras, but just in case you have forgotten them, they are as follows:

The Classical Era: literature of ancient Greece and Rome

Medieval Era: anything written between the 5th and 14th centuries A.D.

Renaissance Era: Known in England as the Elizabethan era. The 14th-16th centuries, depending upon which country.

The Restoration: Refers to dramas written in England between 1660 and 1800.

The Age of Reason: Also called the Enlightenment and in England, the Neo-Classical Era. Generally, the 17th and 18th centuries, but in England 1660-1800.

Romantic Movement: In England, ca. 1800-1830; in the U.S. 1800-1865; in Europe, depending on the country, 1800 to anywhere from 1850 to 1900.

Victorian Era: In England only. 1830-1900.

Realism: In the U.S. from about 1865 to 1900. In Europe as early as 1850 to as late as 1900.

Naturalism: In the U.S. 1870-1900. In Europe, about the same.

Modern Era: Generally, the 20th century.

Note that because cultural changes do not affect every country at the same time, the same era begins and ends at different times depending on which country you are in.

A few of the more famous era books are:

Bernbaum, *A Guide Through the Romantic Movement*
Bowra, *The Romantic Imagination*
Tillyard, *The Elizabethan World View*
Buckley, *The Victorian Temper*
Daiches, *Some Late Victorian Values*

Some books combine the limitations of era with those of a particular genre. Thus one gets books such as:

Edel, *The Modern Psychological Novel*
Daiches, *The Novel & The Modern World.*

It is not important to decide in which category books these are. They may equally well be identified as genre or era books. What is important is to have a generally good idea of the degree of depth and specificity of critical material that is to be found in each of them. The general principle is, here as in all other cases, the more specific the range or scope of the book, the more detailed and difficult is the criticism.

With this we come to the fourth type of book and arrive at a new level of specificity. A critic who wishes to write more profoundly about his subject than he can in the general history, genre, or era book can afford him, will devote an entire book to the writings of one literary author. These *"author books"* will enable the critic to take a look at some of the minute details of certain or all of the literary works of the author being criticized.

Before listing some outstanding examples of this type of book the reader should be made aware that there are two series of author books which are generally of great value to the researcher. The first of these is entitled: *Twentieth Century Views* and is published by Prentice-Hall. There are about thirty-five titles currently available in this series and each of the books is so valuable as to demand the attention of every researcher. Each book contains a series of essays, some of them published previously in scholarly journals, and each essay is written by a different author. Each book is edited by one person, also a specialist in the particular subject, who is responsible for collecting the various essays that have gone into the book. In addition, the editor writes an introduction to the books which usually consists of a brief overview of criticism to be found in the book. The books in this series are, therefore, referred to by editor and title. Thus, for example,

Coburn, ed., *Twentieth Century View Coleridge.*

Another series, not as consistently as good, but containing some very good titles, is published by Noonday Press and is titled *A Reader's Guide to - - - -* (author's name). Unlike the *Twentieth Century Views* each book in the Noonday series is authored by only one person. Thus, for example,

Tindall, *A Reader's Guide to James Joyce.*

In addition, this series contains material of a more simple and introductory nature and, therefore, should be consulted before looking into the *Twentieth Century View* series.

Author books (remember this is a metaphor for books about the author's **works**) may be made even more specific by taking a biographical or historical view of the works. This type of book explores the biography of the author in an attempt to shed some light on the works he has written, and it is called a *Critical Biography*. Frequently, the title of the book will include the words "critical biography," such as Arvin's book *Herman Melville, A Critical Biography*. All too often, however, the title will just indicate the author being criticized and it is left to the reader to peruse the book before he can decide the nature of its contents. Of course, the critical biography will be of primary interest only to the student who is taking a historical approach to the literary work he is writing about.

There are too many fine author books to list even a basic selection of them. Almost every one of the hundreds of famous authors have had at least one worthwhile book devoted to him by some notable critic. The student will be given a method for determining how to find the really good books in the section of the notes entitled "bibliography."

With this we come to the last type of book, the most specific of all critical works: the book devoted to the criticizing of only one literary work. As with the author books there are some famous series the researcher should be acquainted with. The first of these is once again published by Prentice-Hall and the reader should take care not to confuse the two series. The individual work series is called *Twentieth Century Interpreta-*

tions. Like the *Twentieth Century Views* series it consists of a group of some forty books, each one containing essays by different authors and having a single editor. Thus, for example:

> Boulger, ed., *Twentieth Century Interpretations of*
> *"The Rime of the Ancient Mariner."*

We will refer to this type of book as the *"Individual Work"* book. Two other famous series represent a special type of individual work book. This type combines the primary source, i.e., the work of literature itself, with several essays of criticism about the work and is called a *"critical edition."* The two series alluded to above are both critical edition series. The first of these is *The Viking Critical Library,* published by Viking Press. An example is:

> Anderson, ed., *James Joyce: "A Portrait of the Artist as a*
> *Young Man," Text, Criticism, and Notes.*

Note that the title of the book indicates that it is both a copy of the literary work itself (the text) and criticism of the text. The other famous critical edition series is the *Norton Critical Editions* published by Norton Press. In each of these critical editions series the criticism consists of very specific essays, authored by various people, and edited by one man for each particular book.

As with author books the number of individual work books that are worthwhile is too vast to begin enumerating here. With the description of the fifth type of book categorized according to its scope we come to the end of some basic ideas about the type of criticism that is available to the researcher. The reader is now ready to embark upon the gathering of a critical bibliography.

Assignment: To be given at the end of section on bibliography work.

Review Questions:

1. Name and define the five categories or types of books according to their scope.

2.   What are two famous author series?
3.   What is a "critical biography"?
4.   Name three famous individual work series.
5.   What is a "critical edition"?
6.   Can you give examples of all of the above?

4
Bibliography Work

DEFINITIONS AND TYPES
OF BIBLIOGRAPHIES

A bibliography is nothing more than a list of books. Thus a critical bibliography is a list of books of criticism. There are two specific types of critical bibliographies that the reader should be familiar with. The first of these is the *"Selected Bibliography."* This is exactly what the name implies. Some critic has taken the trouble to select certain books on a given topic which he thinks are of special interest to the researcher. Obviously this type of bibliography is most useful since it is one way in which the novice can discover which are the best books in the field. If, for example, one is working on the author Melville and finds that three selected bibliographies list the same two books, then the researcher can be fairly sure that these two books are among the better books about Melville.

A type of bibliography even better is the *"discursive bibliography."* This type discusses the contents and value of the books listed. Consulting a bibliography of this type, therefore, saves the researcher a lot of leg work hunting down books which are eventually found to be of little relevance or value to the researcher's topic.

THE BIBLIOGRAPHY SEARCH

Where can you find ready made bibliographies?

Bibliographies are often to be found at the end of encyclopedia articles and at the end of books of criticism, especially among the books in the author and individual work series mentioned under types of critical books.

Constructing a bibliography does not stop with copying a ready made bibliography out of some book. First, depending on the age of the bibliography you are consulting, the list may not include the latest books on the subject. Secondly, it is one thing to have a list of books on the subject, but quite another to have a list of books that you know are available to you for actual study. Bibliography work, therefore, includes knowing where to get hold of the books, how to construct one's own bibliography, and how to evaluate the quality of the books that are available to you.

Books may be either bought or taken on loan from libraries. First, make use of your own school library. Once inside the library follow this simple procedure to find the books you need:

1. **Check the card catalog for the available books.** Look at title cards in the catalog to see if there are any critical works about the literary work itself. Then check under the author's name to see if there are any books about the author (his works) in general.

   In addition, check the subject cards in the catalog under the three general headings of the era, genre, and country to which your primary source belongs.

   Note: If you are unsure of the general categories that your primary source belongs to, check the encyclopedia for this elementary information, then proceed as indicated.

   An example will illustrate. If the primary source is *Moby Dick,* checking with the encyclopedia will indicate that it is an American novel written in the Romantic era. In the card catalog then look under the general headings "American Literature," "Novel," and "Romanticism," in addition to looking under the more specific headings "Melville" and *"Moby Dick."*

2. Once you have amassed a list of books from card catalog listings, **find out if the library actually has the books** by checking the three areas where books can be found: the circulation shelves, the reference shelves, and the reserve shelves.

    The last two areas contain books which have either limited or no circulation depending on the rules of the particular library. In particular, the reserve shelves contain books that specific instructors have asked the library to set aside so that many students can get to use the books while in the library. There is usually a special list of the books on reserve somewhere near the check out desk and the books are listed under the name of the teacher who placed them on reserve. It pays to get to know all the teachers in the school teaching in the same subject area because perhaps a teacher you do not currently have in that subject has placed a book on reserve that you need. Anyone may use the books on reserve whether or not he is enrolled in the course of the instructor who placed any of them on reserve.

    However, first check the circulation shelves. If the book is not there, then check the reference shelves. Finally, if you have not located the book, check the reserve shelves' list.

    If the book is temporarily out of the library you may reserve it for a small charge, but keep in mind that if you are working on a limited time basis you will probably not have enough time to wait for somebody to return the book and, therefore, you should make attempts at getting the book elsewhere.

If your school library does not have all the books you need to do a satisfactory research job, and this is frequently the case because of the demand for books during the school year, consult other libraries. You should know that almost any college library will allow you to use its facilities if you request such with its librarian. The usual arrangement is that you can use their books as reference, but may not circulate them, so give yourself plenty of time when planning on making a trip to another school's library.

The Public Library is another valuable source of books. You should know some basic information about the Public Library if you live in the New York City area:

1. There are three separate library systems: "The New York Public Library" (Manhattan, Bronx, and Staten Island), the "Queensborough Library" and "The Brooklyn Public Library." You need a different card for each of these systems, but with a card for a particular system you can use any branch within the system. (See telephone directory for a list of the branches.) Anyone may get a library card to any public library as long as he has proof of legal address at the time of applying for it. A telephone, electricity, or gas bill is always acceptable.

2. If you are just searching for one book, save yourself a lot of leg work and call before going. Ask the librarian to see if the book is "on the shelf" and to set it aside for you till you come in. This is a service without charge.

3. Certain branches of the library are superior to others:

   a. In Queens, the best library is the main branch in Jamaica.

   b. In Manhattan, the "Mid-Manhattan Library" at 40th Street just east of Fifth Avenue is generally very good. For the best collection on the performing arts, which includes books about drama, the very best library is the "Library for the Performing Arts" at Lincoln Center (Broadway and 65th Street).

4. Each library system has what is called the "Union Card Catalog." This catalog lists every book in the system and indicates which branch or branches it is available at. An enormous amount of time can be saved by calling this catalog, which is usually located in the building with the main branch, and finding out which libraries in the system have the book or books you are looking for.

5. Once inside a particular library, follow the same procedure that was outlined under using your own school library.

In spite of the very good libraries that students have available to them in this area it is occasionally necessary to purchase a book that cannot be found in the library. Every student should be familiar with what is probably the most famous bookstore in the world. Its name is Barnes & Noble. It is located at Fifth Avenue and 18th Street in Manhattan and specializes in college textbooks and books in all academic subjects. Its paperback section is remarkably complete and the Barnes & Noble annex, across the street from the main store, sells paperbacks at half the list price. If you can't find what you are looking for there, ask one of the generally knowledgeable sales clerks for suggestions about where you may obtain the book.

HOW TO JUDGE THE VALUE
OF CRITICAL BOOKS

There is little point to writing a paper by researching books of questionable value. The sincere researcher must discover, therefore, within the limits of possibility, if the books he is able to obtain are of any real merit. There are several ways to find out if a book is good. First, look for selected or discursive bibliographies. The discursive bibliography might explicitly state the value of the book; whereas the appearance of any book in many selected bibliographies is an indication of the book's value.

Secondly, consult the reference series called **Book Review Digest**. Each year a volume is published containing reviews which appeared originally in many different periodicals. The reviews are of books which were published either that year or the year before. Find out the copyright date of the book you are interested in by looking on the reverse side of the title page, then look in *Book Review Digest* of the same year and of the following year to see if it contains any reviews of that book. The digest is a standard reference work and can be found in almost every library.

Another way to find out a book's value is to consult the back cover of the paperback edition of the book. Often the publisher will quote from reviews if they are favorable. Be careful here to not be persuaded by such quotes as "Excellent" and the like. Such single words might have appeared in the review in praise of something as insignificant as the book jacket rather than the contents of the book.

WRITING UP THE BIBLIOGRAPHY CARD

Writing up an absolutely accurate bibliography card is necessary because the documentation of footnotes of the research paper will largely be taken from the bibliography card. Note very carefully the sample bibliography card on the next page with the explanation that follows. Then write up a similar card for each book as you add it to your bibliography. The following card consists of:

1. The source of the book in upper left-hand corner. If from a library, give the library number. If some other source, give abbreviated code. This enables you to know

882.3D   1

David Daiches, <u>A</u> <u>Critical</u> <u>History</u> <u>of</u> <u>English</u> <u>Literature</u>, <u>Vol. 1</u>,
N. Y., Ronald Press, 1961

pp. 250-262, 282-95

where the book can be obtained if you do not intend to use it immediately if you must return it before you are finished with it.

2. An arbitrary number system in upper right-hand corner. Begin by placing the number one on the first card you write up, number two on the second, etc. This numbering system will relate to the note cards which will be discussed later.

3. The main entry consists of the following information about the book:

   a. The author's name in full, first name first.

   b. The full title of the book, including sub-title and volume number, if any. This should be underlined.

   c. The city of publication. This is usually indicated on the title page of the book. If it isn't you must look in a reference book in the library called **Books in Print**, where you will find a list of all publishers with their addresses. If two or more cities are listed as the places of publication select the one nearest to you.

d. The publisher's name. Do not include "Company," "Inc.," "Press," and the like unless necessary.

e. The copyright date. State the last copyright date which indicates how new the material in the book is. Do not confuse this date with the printing dates which just indicate that more copies were printed. Do not write "copyright" or anything other than the date itself.

f. Near the bottom of the card, indicate the main pages in the book that are related to your topic. Find out which pages these are by consulting the index of the book. The page numbers will show how useful the book is.

g. Note that every item in the main entry is separated by commas only.

h. If a book is an anthology, i.e., a collection of essays, and has more than one author, it will then have an editor who is responsible for putting the book together. When you first write a bibliography card for such a book you will not know which essays you are going to read, so make out a card for the entire book, but be careful to indicate after the editor's name that he is the editor.

e.g. Mark Van Doren, ed., <u>Hawthorne</u>: <u>A</u> <u>Collection</u> <u>of</u> <u>Critical</u> <u>Essays</u>, Englewood Cliffs, N.J., Prentice Hall, 1965

The anthologies will in most cases be books of a more specific nature such as the author book in the example. By the time you get to taking notes from that kind of book you should know which approach you are taking to your topic and, therefore, which essays in the book you will be reading and taking notes from. Once you have decided this, you must make up a separate bibliography card for each of the essays that you use. The card will be a little more complicated than a regular entry:

Richard Chase, "The Trying-Out of the Whale," Melville: A Collection of Critical Essays, ed. Arvin Newton, Englewood Cliffs, N.J., Prentice Hall, 1970

Note the order of information in the above entry:

1. the name of the author of the particular essay
2. the title of the essay in quotation marks
3. the title of the book, underlined
4. the editor's name, this time prefixed by "ed."
5. the three standard publication data.

If you use five essays from this book you must make out five bibliography cards. This is the only way it is possible to write footnotes which give the author of the essay credit for the ideas that you will be using.

Write up these new cards before you do the note taking so that you won't forget and in order to have a different bibliography card number for each different author.

   i.   The card should be three by five inches with lines.

Assignment: Construct a bibliography of critical books relating
#3   to your topic. The list should contain a minimum of ten books and, whenever possible, should contain two books from each of the five kinds of books according to their scope; i.e. two general histories of literature, two genre books, etc.

Review Questions:

1. Where should one look for ready made bibliographies?

2. Under which headings should one look in the card catalog to find books relating to a given topic?

3. What are the three places within the library that books may be found?

4. How many library systems exist in N.Y. City and how does one obtain a card for each system?

5. What is the "Union Card Catalog"?

6. What should be included on the bibliography card and why?

7. How can you find out if a particular book is really good?

5

How to Take Notes

Once you have completed the bibliography search you are ready to begin taking notes from the books which will be the basis for your research paper. Follow the instructions exactly as indicated and you will have something valuable to base your paper on.

Note cards should be four by six inches and ruled. The size is important because it is a good indicator of how long the average note should be. Begin reading the books in your bibliography, reading the most general books first and working your way to the most specific books. Take down any idea that you read that seems to be of value. Remember you are looking for criticism, not evaluation. Criticism is the analysis of a work; evaluation is how good a work it is.

Place only one idea on a card, no matter how short or long it is. If you use up the front of the card and have not finished taking down the idea, suspect that you have more than one idea on the card. Taking down one idea and one idea only might require a bit of practice for some novice researchers, but don't get discouraged. Ask your instructor for help on this if you are not sure of yourself. He can at least look at a few of the cards and let you know if they have only one idea on them.

The idea that you take from any source should be in the form of a direct quote. Some research paper guides will tell you to paraphrase, i.e. put into your own words, the ideas you are noting, but this is not a good procedure because you are never sure once you have returned a book to the library or from wherever you got it if you didn't distort the idea in paraphrasing it. A direct quote allows you to go back to the original source: the author's words themselves, if you have need to.

As you take notes decide as soon as possible, but not later than working on the more general books, i.e. books in scope categories one to three, which critical approach you will use in your paper. If you do this before you get to the longer readings in the more specifically focused books you can then read only those sections which pertain to your particular critical approach and thus relieve yourself of a great deal of useless reading and notetaking. Base your decision on a combination of your own personal evaluation as to which approach is most suitable to the work and on what you have read of the critics thus far. If, for example, the critics seem to favor only a psychological approach to a given work, it would be foolish to take another approach since researching it might be difficult if not impossible.

You may begin quoting in the middle of a sentence or end your quote before the sentence ends that you are quoting from, but if there is information in the middle of a sentence which is not essential to you, you may omit it only by putting in an elipsis (three dots one space apart): . . . . There may be more than one elipsis in a quote if necessary.

e.g.:   "Swinburne took from Sade the idea that God smites equally the just and unjust . . . also the other idea that pain and death are everywhere in nature, . . . and the conception of God as a supreme wickedness . . . and the revolt of man against the divinity he disowns."
from John Schulz, *The Splendid Era,* p. 117

If you have left something out of the middle of the quote, it may not make sense unless you add a few words. If you add anything of your own to a quote, your words must be placed in brackets: [ ] , not parentheses. If you are quoting something that is already a quote, you must use single quotation marks for the quote within the quote.

As you take notes you may find that different critics repeat the same idea. It is not necessary to note the same idea more than once unless the idea is so unusual that you will need to refer the reader of your paper to more than one source to justify the idea, or unless you think you may want to base a generalization on many critics saying the same thing. Do not take notes which consist of generally known facts rather than real critical information.

In addition to any information already given about what the note card should look like: The upper right-hand corner of the note card should contain the same number as appears in this corner on the bibliography card of the book from which you have just taken the information. This saves the job of writing the title and author of the idea on every note card. Begin your quote two lines from the top, leaving room for a topic at the top of the card and on the line immediately following the quote place the page number or numbers from which the quote was taken. Lastly, after taking a note from a source, make a one to three word topic indicating the substance of the note and place this at the top of the card

NOTE: The reason for some of the procedures just mentioned may not seem immediately apparent to you, but as you move into the next stages of writing the paper, namely the arranging of the note cards and the actual writing of the paper, the wisdom behind the use of each procedure will become clear.

Assignment: #4   A safe bet for the taking of notes is to have five notes for each page of the paper that you plan to write. For a paper of five pages, for example, you must take a minimum of twenty-five notes. These notes should be as evenly dispersed as possible among the five kinds of books.

Review Questions:

1.   Which books should be consulted first when beginning to take notes?

2.   How many ideas should be placed on a card and what has this to do with the size of the card?

3.   What form should the idea take and why?

4.   When is the latest you should decide which critical approach to take and why?

5.   How do you delete or add material from a quote?

6.   When should you note the same idea more than once?

7.   What does the note card contain in addition to the note itself?

6

How to Organize
the Note Cards

When you think you have sufficient material with which to write
a paper, you are ready to stop taking notes and begin organizing
them. Once the notes are organized in the following manner,
the entire paper will be structured. The composition of the
paper will then consist of translating the quotes on the cards
into your own language and adding the technical information
required to document your research.

First, check to see that each note card is tagged with a
meaningful topic heading. The topics should be specific. Avoid
or correct general headings such as "character." Instead, indicate
exactly the information on the card: "characters are cynical"
or whatever. Secondly, as you read through the topic headings,
check to see that they suggest the approach that you have chosen to take in the paper. If they do not do this, check to see if,
in general, they suggest a different approach. If no approach is
suggested by the cards, one of two difficulties exist. Either you
did not topic them correctly; in which case reread them trying
to topic them with headings that suggest the approach that you
are using; or, you did not take notes appropriate to the approach
you have selected. This is the greater difficulty to correct, because it means that you must return to notetaking to get more

relevant information. At this point it becomes clear why an approach must be settled on before completing the notetaking process.

Assuming that the topics indicate or can be made to indicate the decided approach, you are ready to begin arranging the cards. Spread out the cards on a large surface so that you can arrange and re-arrange their relative positions. First, begin to group the cards into what's to become the major sub-topics of your paper. Each sub-topic should take up at least as much space as a decent sized composition (ca. two pages). Therefore, in a paper five to seven pages, for example, three to four sub-topics would be ideal. However, since this is probably your first time at researching and writing a paper, adopt the more liberal range of two to five sub-topics. Fewer than two sub-topics would communicate no sense of the complexity and development of the subject to the reader, whereas more than five topics would be just a succession of ideas that were listed rather than explored.

When you have arranged most of the cards into the sub-topic groups there will be some cards that do not fit into the groups. Attempt to make them fit by rereading the cards attempting to retopic them into one of the sub-topic groups. If this does not work, consider these notes irrelevant to your purposes in the paper and place them on the side. The researcher should not be disappointed at having to consider some of his note cards irrelevant. This "blind-alley" work is part of every research project of any kind and the novice researcher must expect a considerable amount of it. If you decided on the approach when you should, the number of irrelevant cards should not exceed ten of the twenty-five cards minimum that you have written. That means you are now down to a minimum number of fifteen cards for a five to seven page paper. If you have fewer than a total of fifteen cards in your sub-topic groups, you must return to notetaking, before you proceed any further, and gather more information. If you find you must do this it will be easier than the first time around since you now know exactly what kind of information you are looking for to add to the paper. If you must return to notetaking do not get discouraged. This backtracking is quite normal, especially for the novice researcher.

At this point it might be beneficial to indicate a few of the possible sub-topic headings that are generally popular with the various approaches. The aesthetic approach deals with the structure of the work, usually analyzing the various elements that compose the work. Sub-topics might, therefore, be an analysis of: (1) plot devices or developmental structure, (2) character types, (3) stylistic characteristics, or (4) use and types of settings. Note that dividing the paper into these sub-topics denotes a very general approach taken in the paper. The paper could just as easily be more specific concentrating, for example, on the characters alone, in which case the sub-topics might be various character types: Romantic characters, Realistic characters, Psychotic characters, etc. Similarly, the paper might focus on style (language) alone and have for its sub-topics certain stylistic devices used by the author.

If you are using an historical approach, the sub-topics might consist of three or four characteristics of the era to which the primary source belongs; thus proving that it is, indeed, a product of its age. An analysis of *The Scarlet Letter,* for example, might consist historically in showing three or four of the Romantic characteristics of the novel. This is one of the easiest types of paper to write and should be given careful consideration by the novice researcher. On the other hand, the paper of this type usually does not say anything that has not already been demonstrated before.

If you are using a psychological approach, the sub-topics might consist in the description of three or four character types or in exploring three or four motivating forces acting upon one or more characters in the literary work. An analysis of *Macbeth,* for example, might consist of showing how Macbeth was motivated by the witches, the meterological environment, the rebellious political environment, and, fourthly, by Lady Macbeth.

These four motivating forces acting upon Macbeth would become the four sub-topics of the paper and demonstrate the general thesis that Macbeth was not free or morally responsible for what he did.

A theological approach might result in sub-topics which explore the degree of absoluteness with which the ultimate being controls the universe and/or in the characteristics which describe the relationship between man and the ultimate. Similarly, an ethical approach might focus on a few of the ethical ideals elaborated by the literary work, or might indicate the effects of moral or immoral behavior.

It would seem that the psychoanalytic approach is the one most difficult to take in a paper based solely upon the student's research, since not enough criticism has been written from this critical point of view as yet. This approach, therefore, becomes an excellent choice when writing a more original "term-paper," rather than in the present assignment which is designed to introduce the student to the basics of research.

To return to the subject of organizing the cards, once you have grouped the cards into the sub-topic groups take one group at a time and employ the following procedure. Using the large surface to arrange cards on, begin to arrange the cards into a final order. For this arrangement one of the following bases may be used:

1. **Order of cause and effect.** Some things follow in a nature cause and effect sequence. Perhaps this is the case with the information within the sub-topic groups.

2. **Order of importance:** Place the two most important ideas first and last. These are the places of emphasis in anything. Work your way from both ends toward the middle position, which will be used by the item having the least importance.

3. **Historical or chronological order:** Arrange cards in the same sequence in which the items that they comment on are arranged in the primary source. This arrangement, of course, is the easiest one to do, but it's also the least rational and inventive organization.

4. **Order of generality:** Place the most general ideas (those with the greatest scope) first and last and work your way toward the center which will contain the most specific idea or fact.

These are only a few possible ways to arrange cards. Perhaps you can think of another way more useful to your purposes.

Follow the above procedure for each of the sub-topic groups that you have. When you have finished arranging all the sub-topics, arrange the sub-topics in relation to each other. Use, whenever possible, the same principle of organizing for all of the organizing.

When you have arranged all of the cards that you have, number each card, beginning with number one for the first card. Place this number in the upper left-hand corner of the card. This number lets you know the position of the individual note within the paper should the cards get accidentally rearranged. More importantly, however, this number becomes the basis for the footnote number that will appear in the paper and which will be discussed later.

Assignment: Arrange your note cards according to the proce-
#5   dure outlined above.

Review Questions:

1. Can you explain the steps of the procedure by which the note cards are arranged?

2.   What are some possible bases for the arrangement?

3.   What are some possible sub-topics for the various approaches?

4.   What problems will necessitate returning to notetaking to gather more information?

5.   How should the cards be numbered once they are arranged?

7
Writing the Paper: Composition

Once you have completed arranging the note cards you are ready to begin writing the paper. It is at this point that the process of writing the notes on note cards and that of arranging the note cards before beginning to write the paper begins to pay off. It might be easier to write notes on notebook paper when doing the research, then immediately writing the paper using whichever notes seem most appropriate at the moment. However, the result of using such a procedure is almost in every case a paper that lacks unity or coherence and a logical development. On the other hand, following the procedures outlined above will result in a paper that is both intelligible to and makes its point with the reader.

CONSTRUCTING A TITLE

The title should indicate both the specific approach being used and the specific scope that the paper will have. This is indicated by the inclusion of key words that signal the reader about the paper's contents. Consider, for example, the title: *The Sin and Suffering of Hester in Hawthorne's "The Scarlet Letter."* The words "Sin and Suffering" indicate to the reader that one of three approaches is being used: the psychological (suffering), or the ethical or theological (sin). Note that it is often impossible to select a word or words that denote one and only one approach. In addition to signaling the approach, *of Hester in Hawthorne's "The Scarlet Letter,"* indicates the specific focus of the paper: "Hester," as well as the more general focus: "Hawthorne's 'The Scarlet Letter'." Note that the general focus indication includes the name of both the author and the work being analyzed in the paper. A good title, therefore, should give the reader a really good idea of what he can expect to find in the paper.

WRITING THE INTRODUCTION

The size of the introduction will depend upon the size of the paper. In a paper of five to seven pages in length, the introduction should be one to two paragraphs long. The purpose of the introduction is twofold. First, it should indicate to the reader the scope and purpose of the paper. The purpose or thesis of the paper is what one hopes to demonstrate by the paper. For example, and historical paper on *Moby Dick* might indicate that "The purpose of this paper is to demonstrate that Melville's novel is among the finest and most obvious examples of American Romanticism"; or a psychological approach to *Macbeth* might state: "The purpose of this paper is" or "I hope to show in this paper that Macbeth is more sinned against than sinning because of the several forces acting upon him which force him to do his 'bloody deeds'."

The scope of the paper is also elaborated on in the introduction by indicating the principal ideas to be covered by the paper. These ideas are the sub-topics that have already been delineated in the arranging of the note cards. The writer of the *Macbeth* introduction started above, therefore, might continue: "The paper will include, therefore, an analysis of the environment in which Macbeth lives, as well as the prophecy of the witches and the urgings and intimidations of his wife, Lady Macbeth."

The second and equally important purpose of the introduction is to justify both the scope and approach of the paper. You must attempt to convince the reader that the specific topic you have selected, the scope, and the point of view you are taking, the critical approach, are worthwhile and worth his attention. Some possible rationales that you might offer the reader are that you are focusing on the most interesting facet of the work, or on the most basic facet of the work, or on the most controversial facet of the work, or on the most representative facet of the work. Be honest with your reader. If part of your rationale is that you can only cover one aspect of the literary work due to limitations of space (the size of the paper), or due to your own limitations as a novice researcher, say so. The rationale you state may be any of those listed, or any that you can come up with, or, may be a combination of several reasons. The idea is that your reader should know, by the time he finishes your introduction, not only what the paper will cover but why it will cover the particular subject with which it is concerned.

THE BODY OF THE PAPER

You might wish to use a note card in your introduction if you can find one that is appropriate to your purposes there. Otherwise, you should begin using your notes at this time. Use the ideas in the order in which they are already organized, paraphrasing most of the ideas. The translating of the language of the various authors you have quoted in the notes into your own language guarantees the stylistic unity of the paper. Use a direct quote of the material on your note cards only if the idea is so important that you wish to emphasize this by quoting the author's language, or, because it is impossible to adequately translate the idea into your own words. In any case use no more than one-third of the ideas as direct quotes.

As you use each of the critical ideas on your note cards add clarity to the ideas by further explanation if necessary. This is especially necessary if the idea contains any special terms that need explanation. Your elaboration of the idea not only guarantees that you will write something that is intelligible to the reader, but also provides legitimate padding for the paper.

As you use the ideas provide a language lead for many of them. If quoting or using an idea of Arvin from his book about *Moby Dick,* you can state: "As Arvin indicates . . ."; or, when making a generalization based upon the ideas of many critics state something to the effect of: "As most critics agree . . .". Reference to where you got the idea, even though you will have to indicate this again in the footnotes, will add a feeling of authority to what you have to say in the body of the paper.

Refer, either by direct quote, or by indirect reference, to the primary source whenever appropriate. Use of the primary source in the paper may help to clarify the ideas of the critics or to convince the reader of the critics' ideas by illustrating their truth, as well as add additional length to the paper.

THE CONCLUSION

The conclusion should be about the same length as the introduction. The function of the conclusion is not simply to re-state what the introduction or the body of the paper has said. Any good researcher in any subject knows that the final word about any subject is never said. The conclusion should, therefore, not really close the subject in the reader's mind, but, instead, stimulate the reader to further thinking about the subject. One way to both stimulate the reader to further investigation of the subject and to lend a greater degree of importance to your paper than it actually has, is to propose a hypothesis in the conclusion that is more general than the particular subject you have proven to be true in the paper. An example will illustrate. "Therefore, we *might* conclude that Hawthorne's principal preoccupation *seems* to be with a constellation of ideas that *might* be variously termed 'theological' or 'ethical' or 'psychological,' since knowledge, which has been the chief consideration of this paper, is indigenous to all three of these disciplines." In this conclusion the writer has indicated or hypothesized something he did not prove in his paper, namely, what Hawthorne's chief preoccupation might be. The paper did, however, reach some conclusions about Hawthorne's interest in human knowing and it is on the basis of that conclusion that the hypothesis was made. Now the reader has been presented with a problem not solved by the paper and is, thus, stimulated to further thinking and/or reading on the subject. Note the emphasized language of the conclusion. Since the writer is only hypothesizing about an idea the language should indicate the tentative nature of the idea.

STYLISTIC CONSIDERATIONS

Some writers are able to concern themselves with both the content and the style or form of their work at the same time. Many others, however, do not wish to divide their attention between content and form while trying to put the content on paper. Proceed, therefore, according to your own abilities in this matter, but you should know that it is easier to write out the content of the paper first, then go back and brush up the style.

The style of a research paper is of particular importance since you do not wish your paper to sound like a bunch of ideas from various sources just thrown together. Attention to matters of style guarantees a paper that is coherent and intelligible.

Among the most important stylistic techniques is the use of transitional words and phrases. Use of these allows for a smooth flowing argument which indicates the relationships that exist between the ideas presented to the reader. There are three basic relationships between ideas: addition, contrast, and cause and effect. Words such as "and," "also," "in addition to," "moreover," "first," "secondly," "finally," and the like indicate a simple addition of ideas. Words and phrases indicating contrast include: "but," "however," "on the other hand," and the like. Cause and effect indicates a sequence where the effect is a conclusion or always follows from the cause. Such words or phrases as "therefore," "thus," "in conclusion," and "consequently" are only a few examples of this type of connecting device.

Consult any good grammar book, such as the Warriner's *English Grammar and Composition,* for a more complete listing of these words so that you can have a fuller range of expression at your command.

A second equally important stylistic device is the matter of paragraph size. The paragraph should be somewhere between five and eight sentences. This is the length needed to state and develop an idea properly. If a visual survey of your completed work indicates that you have written a series of small paragraphs you can suspect that you either did not fully state the ideas contained in the paragraphs, or that you stated only part-ideas and that some of the paragraphs should be combined so that the specifics are integrated into a more general statement of one idea.

Related to paragraph size is the matter of sentence variety. Any composition, especially one of considerable length, should add to its interest value by varying its syntactical structure. This means that there should be present a variety of sentence types: simple, compound, and complex. If most of the sentences within a paragraph are compound or complex, most likely fewer sentences will be needed within that paragraph to make the point fully, whereas a string of simple sentences will have to be more numerous in order to make the same point. This is one reason why there is a range of the number of sentences that can exist in any good paragraph.

Perhaps not as important as the above stylistic matters, but still requiring the attention of any serious writer, is the matter of diction or individual word use. Go through the paper after you have written it weeding out clichés, hackneyed expressions, and colorless vocabulary. Replace these with a vocabulary that is at once interesting and challenging to the reader. If you use any words that you yourself are unfamiliar with, be sure to know their correct usage in order to avoid awkward expressions. A book such as Webster's *Synonyms and Antonyms* or Roget's *Thesaurus* can be consulted for this purpose.

8

Writing the Paper: Mechanics

With the discussion of style we are ready to come to a matter less familiar to the reader, namely, the more mechanical aspects of writing a research paper. Some of the following regulations may seem unnecessarily hair splitting to the casual reader, but they are all of great importance. The implementing of all of the devices to be named will result in a paper that has a positive psychological effect upon the reader. Students often make the mistake of thinking that their instructors operate on a completely rational and non-emotional level. This is certainly unrealistic. An instructor faced with the job of reading a large number of research papers is likely to be in a less than completely positive frame of mind. In most cases he knows that what he will read will not advance his own knowledge, especially if the papers are written by novice researchers. Consequently, the form that the paper has takes on an exaggerated importance. Because of this it is essential that the writer present the reader with as formal and as positive an experience as he can; thus, guaranteeing a positive response in the reader and, consequently, as high a grade as possible on the paper.

Observe the following recommendations with absolute accuracy:

1. Use standard size paper, 8½ by 11, which is clean and fresh.

2. Margins should be one inch on all sides, including top and bottom, except for the left margin, which is one and a half inches to allow room for binding the paper. Paper with the margins already drawn, known as "Thesis Paper," is highly recommended.

3. Typewriter characters should be crisp and clean. Clean the typewriter if necessary. Avoid using so old a machine that the type does not print out in a straight line.

4. Double space the entire paper, except for the title and notes pages which are single spaced with a line skipped between the entries.

5. Bind with three staples one-half inch from left edge of paper and evenly spaced vertically. Staples should be placed in a straight line which will permit the paper to be folded back properly and which will not cut into the paper.

6. The form of the title page:

   a. Title of the paper: one-third from the top and centered and underlined.

   b. Student author's name centered underneath the title.

   c. All other information two-thirds down the page and placed thusly:

   School name   Date
   Course Name   Instructor's last name

7. Form of quotations in the paper:

   a. Place all direct quotations of less than two typewritten lines in length within the text of your paper and surround the quotation with quotation marks. A quotation within a quotation gets single quotation marks.

    b. Quotations of more than two typewritten lines should be single spacing the quotation within itself and indenting it from the margin five spaces on both sides. No quotation marks are necessary since the indentation signals the reader that it is a quote; e.g.

in his book *Herman Melville* Arvin states that:

> Ahab represents the man who cannot tolerate that fact that the universe is a place where one must encounter evil and deal with it in a practical way if one is to survive.[4]

Thus, Arvin . . .

8. Titles in your paper:

    a. Titles of books and full-length plays are underlined.

    b. Titles of poems and short stories are placed in quotation marks.

    c. Titles within titles, such as in the title of your research paper, are placed in quotation marks.

9. Pagination:

    a. Do not count the title page.

    b. Do not number page one of the text of your paper. Begin numbering with the number two on page two.

    c. Place numbers inside the margin with the text, either at top center or top right.

    d. Do not add unnecessary dashes, periods, parentheses, etc. around the page number.

10. Documentation:

    a. Documentation refers to the footnoting system by which you give others credit for their ideas.

    b. Every idea you use in the paper, whether or not you quote the author's language, must be documented.

Therefore, as long as the note card is not your idea you will have one footnote for each note card you use.

c. The footnote number is taken from the note card. It is the number you placed in the upper left-hand corner of the card after you arranged them in the order in which they were to be used in the paper. Therefore, the first idea or note card that you use will have the footnote number one, etc.

d. Placement of footnotes within the text of the paper:

1. Place the footnote number one-half space above the line immediately following the last item of the text; e.g.: said Arvin[1] or, if the end of a sentence: said Arvin.[1]

2. If the idea you are borrowing is stated in the form of a direct quote, the footnote number comes at the end of the quote.

3. If the idea you are borrowing is paraphrased, the footnote number comes at the end of the clause in which the paraphrase appears.

e. Notes Page:

1. All "footnotes" can be placed on the notes page. Some instructors may insist that they be placed at the bottom or foot of each page. This is much more difficult since it requires you leave enough room to put them in after writing the text. It is easier for the reader, however, if he can see the source of the idea on the same page which he is reading.

2. Title this page: <u>Notes</u>:. Place the title in the left-hand corner of the page.

3. Single space within each note entry but skip a line between the entries. Do not indent the entries.

4. For the initial documentation of any source, i.e., the first time you are using an idea-note from a particular book, give all the information about the book that appears on the bibliography card. Duplicate the information exactly as is, beginning with the author's name and including commas. Add to this information the specific page number that the particular idea comes from. This can be found on the note card from which you took the idea.

5. For subsequent documentation of the same source, i.e., anytime after the first time that you are using an idea from the same book, state only the author's last name, followed by a comma and the page number from the note card.

6. There are two exceptions to the form of the documentation for subsequent entries. If you have two or more sources by the same author, follow the author's last name by an abbreviated title, then the page number. Secondly, if the documentation source is the same as in the footnote that immediately precedes it write "Ibid" instead of the author's last name, followed by a comma and the page number.

7. When documenting ideas taken from an anthology, i.e., a book having more than one author, the bibliography card, and thus the footnote, should have all of the following information on it: Author of the essay, first name first; Title of the book, underlined; Editor's name, followed

by "ed."; the three publication data; page number; e.g.:

George Whalley, "The Mariner and the Albatross," Coleridge, <u>A Collection of Critical Essays</u>, Kathleen Coburn, ed., Englewood Cliffs, N. J., Prentice-Hall, 1967, p. 34

8. Refer to Appendix B for the sample Notes Page.

9
After Writing the Paper

You are now ready to perform one last, but very important operation, namely, the proofreading and correcting of the paper after it is typewritten. Proofread the paper twice. Proofread each page after finishing the typing of it. The object here is to catch the large errors that will necessitate rewriting the entire paper if caught too late. Omitting an entire paragraph, for example, might make everything that follows it senseless and the only way to correct it once you have written the entire paper is to rewrite the paper from the point of the mistake onward.

After writing the entire paper, wait at least an hour and proofread for minor errors. The longer you wait before reading the paper the better will be the chance of catching errors. Reading errors immediately after making them we tend to make the same error again. Better still, have someone else, who cannot anticipate what is on the page, proofread for you. He will be able to be more objective and critical while reading.

Make corrections of minor errors by using some type of correct-type product available in every stationary store. Attempting to erase the error generally results in a smudged paper. If omitted words have to be inserted, insert them in the space above the line at the point where they are to be inserted and use a "caret" to indicate the insertion: e.g. "to the ∧of the line."

Print the correction in ink of the same color or type all corrections.

Assignment: Write the paper in sections. The following section
#6 is due in class, handwritten or typewritten, two
days apart:

1. Introduction
2. Sub-topic #1
3. Sub-topic #2
4. Sub-topic #3
5. Sub-topic #4 and #5 (if any)
6. Conclusion
7. Finished typed copy

Review Questions:

1. What should the introduction contain?

2. What should the conclusion contain?

3. What is the function of transitional words
   and phrases and what are some examples of
   the different types of transitional words
   and phrases?

4. What are two other stylistic considerations
   you should be aware of?

5. What is the reason for being exact about
   the mechanical aspects of the paper?

6. What margins, spacing, and pagination
   should the paper have?

7. What is the form of the title page?

8. What two forms may quotations in the
   paper take?

9. What information is present in a footnote
   of an initial entry (name each item)?

10. What three ways are subsequent entries
    documented?

11.   How is an anthology documented?

12.   How many times must one proofread and why?

13.   How does one make corrections in the paper?

Appendix A:
Primary Source List

SUGGESTED LITERARY TOPICS

Aeschylus, *Agamemnon:* Greek Tragedy about the murdering of a war lord by his wife when he returns from the Trojan War.

Aeschylus, *The Libation Bearers:* Greek Tragedy about a son who murders his mother out of revenge (See Agamemnon).

Aeschylus, *Eumenides:* Greek Tragedy which completes the above plays. The trial of the murdering son by the Furies.

Beaumarchais, *The Barber of Seville:* 18th century French comedy displaying both wit and the rise of individualism. Basis for Rossini's famous opera of the same name.

Beaumarchais, *The Marriage of Figaro:* sequel to the above play.

Camus, *The Fall:* 20th century French novel about the condition of Modern Man who denies all beliefs and guideposts for living.

Camus, *The Plague:* Allegory of the French moral degeneration and Nazi occupation during W.W. II. Nobel prize book.

Cervantes, *Don Quixote:* Very long 17th century Spanish novel about the decline of medieval man. Considered one of the world's greatest novels.

Chekhov, *Selected Short Stories:* Late 19th century Russian writer who is most often depressing. Considered one of the greatest short story writers.

Conrad, *Typhoon:* Short but difficult novel of the sea by a master of mood, description, and psychological states of mind.

Dostoyevski, *Crime and Punishment:* Late 19th century Russian novel. Long and difficult study of guilt. Considered one of the greatest novels.

Dostoyevski, *Notes from the Underground:* Short but difficult and tedious description of man's present futile situation. An important work to Existential philosophers.

Euripedes, *Medea:* Greek Tragedy about a wronged and jealous wife who takes a murderous revenge.

Euripedes, *The Trojan Women:* Greek Tragedy focusing on the griefs and defeat of four female victims of the fall of Troy.

Flaubert, *Madame Bovary:* 19th century French novel about a woman's attempt to escape the commonplace world. Considered one of the world's greatest novels.

Gide, *The Immoralist:* 20th century French novel. An undramatic confession of a man who dedicates himself to a subtle form of evil.

Goethe, *Faust:* 19th century German poetic drama. Classic story of a man who sells his soul to the devil. Difficult but one of the most important works ever written.

Golding, *Lord of the Flies:* 20th century British allegory of man's depraved nature. Story of a group of boys stranded on an island and their fall into evil.

Hesse, *Siddhartha:* 20th century novel, allegory, and parable. A short but difficult story of an Indian boy who experiences all things to learn the meaning of life.

Hesse, *Steppenwolf:* Difficult but fascinating novel about the multiple personalities of modern man who struggles for happiness and is disillusioned.

Hesse, *Narcissus & Goldmund:* Allegory, with erotic overtones, of the two sides of the human personality and how they integrate in art. A difficult but superb novel.

Ibsen, *A Doll's House:* 19th century Norwegian drama which is one of the first psychological works about the emancipation of women and the failure of the Romantic ideal.

Ibsen, *Ghosts:* Psychological drama of hypocracy and its moral and physical consequences.

Ibsen, *The Master Builder:* Symbolic statement of man's desire to be his own God.

Ibsen, *The Wild Duck:* Social and psychological drama about people living with necessary illusions and seeing them destroyed.

Ionesco, *The Lesson:* Difficult French Existential drama about man's inability to communicate with man.

Ionesco, *Rhinoceros:* Existential French drama. An allegory and satire on conformity.

Joyce, *A Portrait of the Artist as a Young Man:* 20th century Irish novel. Difficult, stream of consciousness, account of a young man's struggle to find something of value. One of the world's greatest novels.

Malory, *Le Morte D'Arthur:* 15th century British telling of the Arthurian legends. Long and difficult but quite interesting.

Mann, *Confessions of Felix Krull, Confidence Man:* 20th century German novel about a handsome, clever rogue who sees the world as something created for his entertainment.

Moliere, *The Miser:* 17th century French dramatic satire about a man who finds his family getting in the way of his greater love: money.

Racine, *Phaedra:* 17th century French tragedy based upon the Greek legend of incest and villainy.

Shaw, *Arms and the Man:* 20th century Irish satire on war, politics, and idealism.

Shaw, *St. Joan:* 20th century retelling of the martyrdom of Joan of Arc. Shaw uses the story for his own purposes.

Sophocles, *Antigone:* Greek Tragedy about a woman torn between two obligations. One of the most famous plays ever written.

Virgil, *The Aeneid:* Roman epic poem modelled after Homer about Aeneas who incorporates all the virtues considered typically Roman. One of the world's greatest works.

Voltaire, *Candide:* 18th century French satire on the Enlightenment belief that this is "the best of all possible worlds." One of the most important and entertaining criticisms of the Enlightenment.

Twain, *Huckleberry Finn:* 19th century American novel which is both realistic and allegorical. Considered one of the greatest American novels.

Dickens, *David Copperfield:* Long 19th century British novel about growing into manhood. Considered Dickens' masterpiece.

Swift, *Gulliver's Travels:* 18th century satirical novel about the pet ideas of the Enlightenment.

Steinbeck, *The Grapes of Wrath:* 20th century American novel depicting the depressing story of migrant farm workers during the depression of the 1930's.

Hawthorne, *The Scarlet Letter:* 19th century American novel about Puritan hypocrasy. Difficult but one of the greatest.

Crane, *The Red Badge of Courage:* Late 19th century American novel which portrays the discrepancy between appearance and reality.

Poe, *Tales:* Some of the best short stories ever written usually exploring abnormal psychology. Considered by many the greatest short story writer.

Austen, *Pride and Prejudice:* 19th century British novel of manners and mores of the middle class. Beautifully written but somewhat tame.

Melville, *Moby Dick:* 19th century American novel. Long, difficult, profound, Romantically imaginative. Among the greatest novels ever written.

Huxley, *Brave New World:* 20th century British. Difficult but brilliant novel about a futuristic society where individualism is outlawed. The best sci-fi novel ever written.

Bronte, *Jane Eyre:* 19th century British Romantic novel about love overcoming every physical and social obstacle.

Wilder, *Our Town:* Warm 20th century American drama about family life, human relationships, and value beyond death.

Bronte, *Wuthering Heights:* 19th century Romantic British novel about strong personalities and a strong love affair.

Hardy, *Return of the Native:* Late 19th century British novel examining social problems from a psychological and somewhat depressing point of view.

Dickens, *Great Expectations:* 19th century British novel about growing up and finding what is really important in life.

Conrad, *Heart of Darkness:* 20th century British novel. Short but difficult tale probing the more negative aspects of the human personality.

Conrad, *Lord Jim:* 20th century British novel. Psychological novel that stresses the mystery of the human personality as a source of good and evil. Difficult, but considered one of the greatest novels.

James, *Turn of the Screw:* 19th century psychological short story. A ghost story that raises the question about the reality of the ghost. Short, but difficult.

O'Neill, *A Long Day's Journey into Night:* 20th century American drama. Depressing autobiographical sketch of the dramatist's early family life.

Faulkner, *As I Lay Dying:* 20th century American novel. Short but difficult story of the transportation of a mother's body and the thoughts it provokes in the people on the journey to the burial site.

Shakespeare, *Macbeth:* Renaissance drama of crime, guilt, and punishment. One of the greatest dramas ever written.

Shakespeare, *Measure for Measure:* A problem play, mixing humor and drama, about the administering of Law with mercy.

Shakespeare, *King Lear:* One of the world's greatest plays. About the meaning of human suffering and good and evil. Difficult, but a masterpiece.

Shakespeare, *Othello:* A study in jealousy. One of Shakespeare's four most famous dramas.

Shakespeare, *The Tempest:* Shakespeare's last play. A comedy with serious philosophical implications. Difficult but brilliant.

Chaucer, *Canterbury Tales:* Earliest poetic masterpiece in the English language. Great critique of medieval society.

Blake, *Poems:* British Romantic poet considered the best by many. Easy to read but profound in meaning, Blake explores the psychological nature of good and evil and of reality.

Wordsworth, *Immortality Ode:* Romantic poem of considerable length which concerns most of the ideology of the Romantics.

Coleridge, *The Rime of the Ancient Mariner:* The supreme masterpiece of Romantic poetry, containing profound psychological insights.

Keats, *Selected Poems:* Difficult Romantic British poet whose language and imagery, as well as ideas, have not been surpassed.

Shelley, *Selected Poems:* Another British Romantic. Very difficult but profound poet influenced by the Greek philosopher Plato.

Tennyson, *Idylls of the King:* Lengthy 19th century narrative poem of the Arthurian legend used to allegorically discuss 19th century moral problems.

Browning, *Selected Dramatic Monologues:* Late 19th century British poet who demonstrates the meanness of man.

Melville, *Billy Budd:* Short but very difficult 19th century American novel about good, evil, and Law. A masterpiece.

Fielding, *Tom Jones:* Very long but easy to read 18th century British novel which satirizes manners and morals of the time.

Defoe, *Moll Flanders:* 18th century British social novel about the effects of the environment upon the human person.

Dickenson, *Selected Poems:* 19th century American poetry about a variety of topics of interest to the Romantics. Somewhat pessimistic but beautifully wrought.

Dante, *The Inferno:* 13th century Italian poetic masterpiece. A difficult epic poem considered one of the very greatest literary works. A description of hell.

Eliot, *The Wasteland:* Difficult 20th century poem about the situation modern man finds himself in. Profound. One of the most influential poems of the 20th century.

Lawrence, *Sons and Lovers:* Long 20th century British novel. A profound story of a working class figure who struggles to attain something of value.

Sartre, *No Exit:* 20th century French Existential drama about three people trapped in hell.

Beckett, *Waiting for Godot:* 20th century French Existential drama considered by many the greatest play of the 20th century. A profound exploration about the meaning of life.

Kafka, *Selected Short Stories:* 20th century Czech writer of the greatest importance. Weird stories about psychological compulsion and the absurdity of life.

Kafka, *The Trial:* Novel about a man placed on trial without knowing why and for what. A profound and frightening portrait of modern man.

Homer, *The Iliad:* Epic masterpiece of the Trojan War and the anger of Achilles. Greek poem considered one of the greatest works ever written. Long and difficult.

Homer, *The Odyssey:* Odysseus' fantastical wandering for ten years on his way home after the fall of Troy. Great poetic masterpiece. Long, but interesting.

Shakespeare, *The Merchant of Venice:* Early comedy with serious overtones which explore the nature of greed and love.

Shakespeare, *A Midsummer Night's Dream:* Early Romantic comedy about love and the meeting of the real world with the Fairy kingdom. Shakespeare's early masterpiece.

Appendix B:
Sample Notes Page

<u>Notes:</u>

1   Martin Esslin, "The Theatre of the Absurd," <u>Theatre</u> <u>in</u> <u>the</u> <u>Twentieth</u> <u>Century</u>, Robert W. Corrigan, ed., N.Y., Grove Press, 1963, p. 244

2   <u>Ibid</u>, p. 229

3   <u>Ibid</u>, p. 230

4   <u>Ibid</u>, p. 231

5   Carolin Riley, <u>Contemporary</u> <u>Literary</u> <u>Criticism,</u> Detroit, Gale Research, Vol. 1, 1973, p. 154

6   <u>Ibid</u>, p. 154

7   <u>Ibid</u>, p. 154

8   Esslin, p. 229

9   Kenneth M. Cameron, <u>A</u> <u>Guide</u> <u>to</u> <u>Theatre</u> <u>Study</u>, N. Y., Macmillan, 1974, p. 190

10 Riley, p. 154

11 Cameron, p. 190

12 John Gassner and Edward Quinn, eds., <u>The</u> <u>Reader's</u> <u>Ency-clopedia</u> <u>of</u> <u>World</u> <u>Drama,</u> N. Y., Crowell, 1969, p. 464

13 Josephine Jacobsen and William R. Mueller, <u>Ionesco</u> <u>and</u> <u>Genet,</u> <u>Playwrights</u> <u>of</u> <u>Silence,</u> N. Y., Hill and Wang, 1968, p. 1

14   Riley, p. 155

15   Ibid, p. 154

16   Martin Esslin, <u>Theatre of the Absurd</u>, Garden City, N. Y.,
      Doubleday, 1961, p. 151

17   Ibid, p. 151

18   Ibid, p. 152

19   Ibid, p. 151

20   Raymond Cowell, <u>Twelve Modern Dramatists,</u> N. Y., Perga-
      mon, 1967, p. 124

21   Cameron, p. 188

22   Esslin, "Theatre of the Absurd," p. 239

23   Jacobsen and Mueller, p. 227